African-American History

Grades 2–3

by

Laura Shallop

Published by Instructional Fair
an imprint of
Frank Schaffer Publications®

Instructional Fair

Author: Laura Shallop
Cover Artist: Larry Johnson
Interior Artist: Chris Wold Dyrud

Frank Schaffer Publications®

Instructional Fair is an imprint of Frank Schaffer Publications.

Send all inquiries to:
Frank Schaffer Publications
8720 Orion Place
Columbus, Ohio 43240

African-American History—Grades 2–3

ISBN: 0-7424-0080-8

12 13 14 15 PAT 12 11 10 09

To the Teacher

Carter G. Woodson, an early twentieth-century scholar, noted that the black experience was glaringly missing from the books he studied. It was as if the African and African-American pasts did not exist. He initiated a dedicated effort to record his people's history and to teach it to the public. In 1926, he started the first Negro History Week. From that event evolved the practice of designating February as Black History Month—a time when the curriculum in American schools highlights black people and events that have had great impact and influence on defining who we are as Americans today.

The twenty-one stories in this activity book make up an inspiring album of Americans of African descent who, against all odds, made significant contributions to American history—to our cultural and political life, to the development of our social and legal thinking, to our economic and technological achievements, and to every other arena in which human progress is measured. Their stories are told simply, in language that is meaningful to the six- to nine-year-old student learning about these notable people and events for the first time. Each story is followed by an activity that will help students recall the major contributions of each subject. We suggest you help students summarize the achievements of each of the subjects. You will want to discuss why each of these people or events was important in history.

To use this book:

- Select the subjects whose stories you will read with your students and copy along with the corresponding worksheet.

- Determine the best way for students to read the material: as a class, in pairs, or in small groups.

- Remember that students will enjoy hearing you elaborate on the stories that are told. Each piece is purposely brief—intended to be read by young children in a short class session. You should enrich the stories by sharing additional information with your students.

- Encourage students to save their activity sheets in a portfolio or a notebook. Give them an opportunity to create their own covers for their booklets. This collection can be saved and used for reading activities at a later date.

- Students love to share their knowledge. Remind them to show these activity pages to their families. This will help the entire family learn about people and events that helped shape American history.

Table of Contents

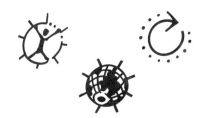

Benjamin Banneker
1731-1806

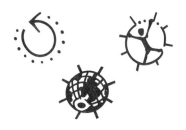

Benjamin Banneker was a very curious child. While other children played, Benjamin would say, "I'd rather read my books."

Benjamin loved to play with numbers. Math was like a puzzle to him. When he was young, he made a large clock. He made it to look like a watch someone had loaned him. For 40 years, the clock kept perfect time.

Years later, Benjamin borrowed a telescope and some books about astronomy. "I've never seen so many stars before," he thought. With these tools, he taught himself all about the stars. Before long, he knew enough to publish an almanac. His almanac was a book that contained weather information, home remedies, poems, and anti-slavery essays. Scientists all over the world learned from Benjamin's almanac.

As Benjamin grew older, he continued to learn new things. For example, he studied surveying. Surveying is measuring the land. He became so respected as a surveyor that President George Washington asked him to help plan our nation's capital, Washington, D.C. Benjamin Banneker was such a great person that a postage stamp was created to honor him in 1980.

Benjamin Banneker–The Stargazer

Write about Benjamin Banneker's main achievements. The picture clues will help you.

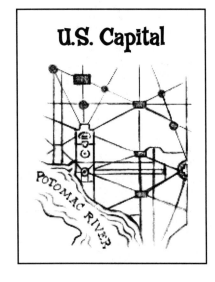

U.S. Capital

1. _____
   _____
   _____
   _____
   _____
   _____
   _____

2. _____
   _____
   _____
   _____
   _____
   _____
   _____

3. _____
   _____
   _____
   _____
   _____
   _____
   _____

Sojourner Truth
1797–1883

Sojourner Truth was born a slave on a plantation in New York. When she was born, her slave master named her Isabella Baumfree. After she escaped from slavery, she decided to change her name to Sojourner Truth. She wanted to tell everyone about the evils of slavery.

Sojourner was a very tall woman with a powerful voice. She was a good speaker. No matter where Sojourner spoke, crowds gathered to listen to her. Even though she could not read or write, she became a famous speaker.

Sojourner spoke all over the North about ending slavery. She criticized slave owners for bad treatment of their slaves. She also spoke about women's rights. She believed that a woman could do a job just as well as a man. In 1851, Sojourner gave her famous speech, "Ain't I a Woman?" She stood in front of a large audience and showed her right arm and her strong muscles. She said, "I have plowed, I have planted, and no man could head me. And ain't I a woman?"

Sojourner Truth spoke out for the freedom of slaves. Slavery was finally outlawed when the Thirteenth Amendment to the Constitution became a law in 1865.

Sojourner Truth: Freedom's Messenger

What were Sojourner Truth's beliefs? Fill in the boxes below.

Sojourner's Beliefs about Slavery

_____

_____

_____

_____

_____

_____

Sojourner's Beliefs about Women

_____

_____

_____

_____

_____

_____

Frederick Douglass
1818–1895

Frederick Douglass was born smart and proud. He found life as a slave unbear-able. Many times he had to fight to get enough food. As a boy, he worked as a servant for a family in Maryland. He was taught to read and write. Once Frederick realized he was not different from any other person, he wanted to escape slavery.

In 1838, Frederick escaped to New York. Because he had been a slave, Frederick was asked to speak at meetings of the Anti-Slavery Society. He became a strong leader and gave great speeches. Some people wondered if Frederick had ever really been a slave because he seemed so well educated. He decided to prove himself by writing a book about his life. He also used his writing talents to start a newspaper, called the *North Star*.

During the Civil War, he encouraged black people to fight for the North. Thousands of African Americans became soldiers in the Union army. In 1863, President Abraham Lincoln invited Frederick to the signing of the Emancipation Proclamation. He was also made a U.S. marshal and was an advisor to five presidents. Near the end of his life, Frederick Douglass became the first African American to be named as a candidate for president of the United States.

A Voice for Freedom

Fill in the time line with important events in Frederick Douglass's life. You may look at the article for help.

1818

1838

1863

Nat Turner Slave Revolt
1831

Many black slaves were willing to risk their lives for freedom. In order to escape, some slaves secretly planned to kill their masters. These were called slave revolts.

Nat Turner led one of the most well-known slave revolts. Nat was the son of an African-born slave in Virginia. He was very bright as a child and always had a vision of being free.

Nat became a successful preacher. In his twenties he came to believe that he was meant to take up arms against slave owners and to free his people. He decided to act on his beliefs. Carefully and quietly, he planned his attack. No one turned him in or revealed his plans.

On August 21, 1831, Nat Turner and a group of slaves armed themselves with hatchets. They planned to murder slave masters. Within 36 hours, they had killed more than 55 people, including the families of the slave masters. They were ready to kill many more, but Nat and his followers were captured and hanged. After this revolt, many slave masters lived in constant fear of revolt.

Nat Turner Revolt Crossword Puzzle

Complete the crossword puzzle. Use the Word Bank and the article for help.

Across

2. an idea in a person's mind
3. Nat was a very _____ child.
5. a planned uprising or rebellion
6. to run away
7. a hope or wish
10. liberty
11. the state where Nat was born
12. people forced to work for no money

Down

1. to free someone
4. a person who leads a church
8. weapons
9. Nat's last name

Word Bank

arms
liberate
Virginia
dream
preacher
vision
escape
bright
freedom
revolt
slaves
Turner

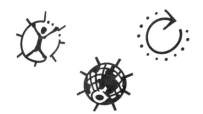

Harriet Tubman
1820-1913

Harriet Tubman was born a slave in Maryland. Her childhood was hard, and she was often beaten. During the day, Harriet worked hard under the hot sun. She became very strong. At night, she planned how she would use the North Star to guide her to freedom. Finally, in 1849, she escaped. But Harriet found no happiness being free. She could not forget the people she had left behind, especially her parents. So Harriet traveled back to the South 19 times to help other slaves escape. This is why she became known as the "Moses of Her People."

Harriet followed a secret escape route called the Underground Railroad. This wasn't a real railroad. It was a series of "stations," or safe places, where slaves hid on their difficult journey North. Often traveling alone, Harriet outsmarted slave trackers. She confused their dogs by sprinkling red pepper along her path. Sometimes she even had to use force to keep frightened runaways from turning back. Harriet helped lead more than 300 slaves to freedom.

During the Civil War, Harriet Tubman served with the Union army. First she was a nurse and then a spy. When she died in 1913, she received full military honors for her courage and service.

The Moses of Her People

What kind of person was Harriet Tubman? Think about the qualities that helped her lead her people to freedom. The words in the boxes may help you. Describe courageous, intelligent, or caring things Harriet did.

Harriet Tubman

Courageous

_____
_____
_____
_____
_____
_____
_____
_____

Intelligent

_____
_____
_____
_____
_____
_____
_____
_____

Caring

_____
_____
_____
_____
_____

Emancipation Proclamation and the 13th, 14th, and 15th Amendments

Thursday, January 1, 1863, was a bright day in Washington, D.C. President Abraham Lincoln had a busy day ahead of him. He had paperwork to do and meetings to go to. Since it was New Year's Day, there would be a party at the White House. Then he had to sign the Emancipation Proclamation. This was a legal paper that would free slaves in all the states that were fighting against the North in the Civil War.

Since 1861, America had been at battle in the Civil War. Many men had already died fighting. President Lincoln wanted to end the war quickly. He knew this would be a very important document. Just before he dipped his pen into the ink, he said, "I never, in my life, felt more certain that I was doing right than I do in signing this paper."

News of the president's action went out across the land. In northern cities, thousands of people sang songs, marched in parades, and listened to speeches. Slaves in the South celebrated with great joy. At last, their long struggle for freedom had been won!

When the Civil War was over, and the slaves were free, there were still many problems to solve. One problem was about the rights of blacks—should they have the same rights as other citizens of the United States? Congress passed three amendments to the Constitution that helped answer this question.

The first of these was the Thirteenth Amendment, which was passed in 1865. This amendment said that there could be no slavery in the United States. It set all slaves free. Three years later, Congress passed the Fourteenth Amendment. It made black people U.S. citizens and gave them equal rights.

In 1870, Congress passed another amendment. The Fifteenth Amendment gave black men the right to vote. It said that all people have the right to vote no matter what race or color they are.

From Slavery to Freedom

Fill in the boxes with your answers to the questions.

What did the Emancipation Proclamation say and why was it important? _____

_____

_____

_____

_____

_____

_____

_____

Write one sentence to tell why each of the following amendments is important.

13th _____

_____

_____

14th _____

_____

_____

15th _____

_____

_____

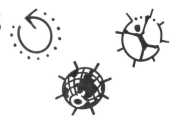

Dr. Daniel Hale Williams
1856–1931

Dr. Daniel Hale Williams graduated from Chicago Medical College in 1883. In 1891, he founded the Provident Hospital in Chicago. It was the first black-owned and black-run hospital in the United States. It was also the first hospital to care for both blacks and whites. Dr. Williams also started the first school for black nurses in the United States.

At Provident Hospital, Dr. Williams performed a daring surgery on July 10, 1893. At that time, no other doctor had ever tried to operate on the human heart. He was taking a big risk. If he failed, his medical license could be taken away, and his hospital could be forced to close. Dr. Williams was sure he would succeed. He cut open the patient's chest and sewed up a tear in the heart. To everyone's amazement, the patient survived. He was soon back to work and lived another 20 years!

All over the world, scientists and doctors read of this amazing operation. Throughout his medical career, Dr. Williams continued to make medical history. His early work in medicine helped make possible many of the heart transplants performed today.

An Amazing Heart Surgeon

Name three achievements of Dr. Daniel Hale Williams. What were the results of those achievements?

Achievement _____

_____

Result _____

_____

Achievement _____

_____

Result _____

_____

Achievement _____

_____

Result _____

_____

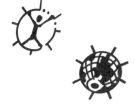

George Washington Carver
1864–1943

George Washington Carver is best known for his work in farming. His ideas helped to improve the quality of life for millions of Americans.

George was born a slave during the Civil War. He was very interested in science and art. He went to the Iowa Agricultural College to study science. After finishing his education, he decided to use his knowledge to help farmers in the South. He moved to Tuskegee, Alabama, to work as a teacher at the Tuskegee Institute of Technology.

For nearly 200 years, Southern farmers had grown only cotton. The soil was weak. Carver knew that the way to make the soil better was to grow different crops each year. This method is called crop rotation. Carver was the first scientist to convince farmers to grow peanuts one year, sweet potatoes the next, and soybeans after that. This new method was a great success. Soon farmers were producing big, healthy crops year after year.

Dr. Carver was a hard-working scientist. He discovered 300 uses for peanuts and 100 for sweet potatoes. He became famous around the world for his creative ideas. In 1943, President Franklin D. Roosevelt had a statue made in Dr. Carver's honor. It was the first national monument dedicated to an African American in U.S. history.

A Scientist Helps Farmers

Fill in the peanut. Tell how George Washington Carver helped farmers.

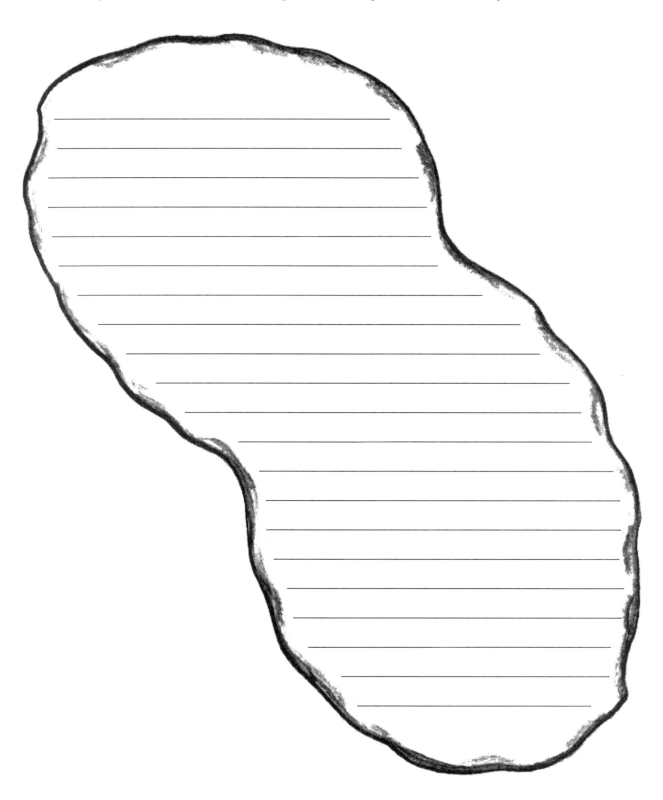

Madam C. J. Walker
1867–1919

Madam C. J. Walker was one of the first American women to become a millionaire.

Madam C. J.'s name was Sarah Breedlove when she was born. She grew up poor and had almost no education. Sarah married very young and had a daughter. When she was only 20, her husband died. To support herself and her daughter, she worked washing other people's clothes.

Sarah then married a man named Charles Walker. She changed her name to Madam C. J. Walker. Madam C. J. had the idea of starting her own business selling hair care products. She created a special hair treatment for African-American women and decided to sell her products door to door. This became known as the "Walker Method." Overnight, she found herself in business, with assistants, schools, and a manufacturing company.

Madam C. J. Walker gave money to many black causes, such as the Frederick Douglass Museum and the National Association for the Advancement of Colored People (NAACP). She often said, "I got my start by giving myself a start." By the end of her life, she had become one of the most successful business-people of her time.

Madam Millioniare

Describe two important events in Madam C. J. Walker's life.

```
_____
_____
_____
_____
_____
_____
```

```
_____
_____
_____
_____
_____
_____
```

Madam C. J. Walker said, "I got my start by giving myself a start."
Name three goals you want to accomplish and how you might do it.

1. _____

_____

2. _____

_____

3. _____

_____

Carter G. Woodson
1875-1950

For many years, the history of African Americans was not recorded in schoolbooks. Carter G. Woodson, the "Father of Black History," was determined to make the facts known.

Carter was the oldest of nine children in a very poor family. To help his family, he worked in the coal mines near his home in Virginia.

Carter was known for his sharp mind. He had a great desire to learn and taught himself to read and write. He went to high school while he was working and finished in a year and a half.

After finishing college, Carter traveled to the Philippines. There he was a supervisor of schools for six years. Back in the United States, Carter moved to Washington, D.C., and became a school principal.

Carter realized that black American history and culture was not in the textbooks he read. He knew that someone had to write about his people's history and teach it to others. It became his dream that "young blacks would grow up with a firm knowledge of their ancestors."

Dr. Carter G. Woodson dedicated his life to recording the history of African Americans. In 1926, he started the first Negro History Week. Today it is known as Black History Month and is celebrated in February of each year.

Father of Black History

Certain conditions in Carter Woodson's life brought about certain effects. For each cause, write about the effects on Carter Woodson's life and attitude.

Cause

Effect

His family
was very poor.

_____
_____
_____
_____
_____

He had a great
desire to learn.

_____
_____
_____
_____
_____
_____
_____

He discovered
that most history books
did not include black history.

_____
_____
_____
_____
_____
_____

Mary McLeod Bethune
1875–1955

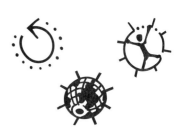

Mary McLeod Bethune came from a family of 22 children. She was the first child in the family born a free person. Her parents said she was a special child, and their words proved true.

At an early age, Mary had a strong desire to learn. But in her hometown in South Carolina, there were no schools for black children. Many people thought that education was a waste of time for black children. When she was 11 years old, a school opened five miles from her home. Mary walked there every day and proved that she was a very good student.

After Mary graduated, she was accepted into college. She dreamed of being a missionary in Africa. She went to Chicago to study at the Moody Bible Institute. As soon as she graduated, she tried to become a missionary but was told she was too young. Mary taught school for a short time instead. She married

Albertus Bethune and had a son. Soon after that, they moved to Florida.

By this time, Mary was a fine teacher, but she wanted to do even more. With about $1.50, she decided to start a school for girls. In the beginning, she used a box for her desk and found her students' chairs in the city dump. Little by little, her school grew until it became Bethune College. By 1923, Bethune College had joined with Cookman Institute. All of Mary's hard work paid off. Today Bethune-Cookman College continues to educate young African-American students.

Get in Step with Mary McLeod Bethune

Name four steps Mary McLeod Bethune took to become a leader in education.

Number 1

_____
_____
_____
_____

Number 2

_____
_____
_____
_____

Number 3

_____
_____
_____
_____

Number 4

_____
_____
_____
_____

The Harlem Renaissance
1920s

The Harlem Renaissance was an important time for black artists and writers. It became known as the "Age of the Greats."

During the late 1890s through the 1920s, many black Americans moved from the South to northern cities. During this time, the population in Harlem, New York grew from 50,000 to 80,000 people. It became the largest community of black Americans in the United States. By the 1920s, blacks in Harlem felt free to express themselves through art and literature. Black artists celebrated their own culture as never before.

Jazz music swept the nation. Black musicians who went north brought their music with them. Among the greatest of these jazz musicians was Louis Armstrong.

There were many great singers as well, such as Marian Anderson and Paul Robeson. The poet Langston Hughes was one of the most talented black writers of the Harlem Renaissance. During this period, other black writers and artists produced novels, operas, dances, and Broadway plays and musicals.

In 1929, the United States entered a time called the Great Depression. Thousands of Americans lost their jobs. There was not enough money for food and other things. The happiness of the Harlem Renaissance came to an end, but the talent of the artists had already made a mark on American culture.

The Age of the Greats

The Harlem Renaissance was an important time for all African-American artists. Answer the questions. Recall some of the greatest musicians, writers, and singers of the time.

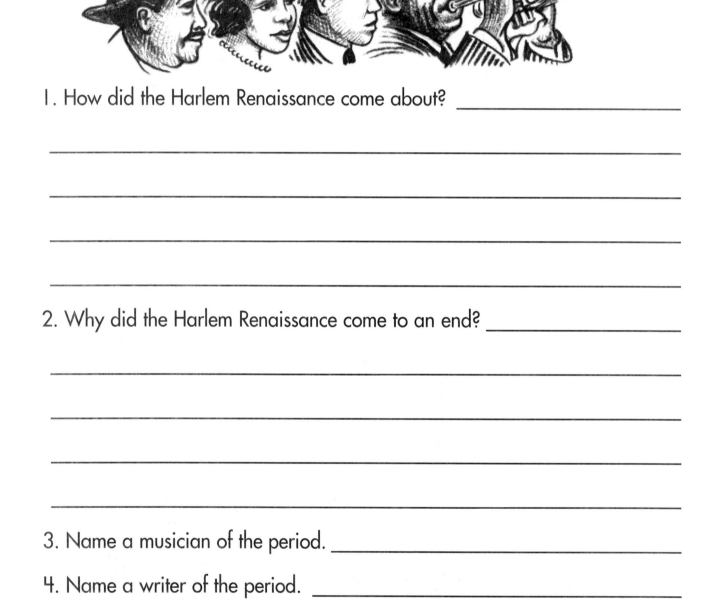

1. How did the Harlem Renaissance come about? _____

_____

_____

_____

_____

2. Why did the Harlem Renaissance come to an end? _____

_____

_____

_____

3. Name a musician of the period. _____

4. Name a writer of the period. _____

5. Name a singer of the period. _____

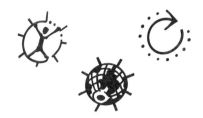

Langston Hughes
1902–1967

Langston Hughes loved to write. He was one of the most loved poets of his time. He also wrote plays, operas, songs, and books.

Langston was born in Joplin, Missouri, and was reared by his mother and grandmother. They moved often, but after his grandmother died, he and his mother settled in Cleveland. Langston was a lonely child and spent most of his time reading. When he was in elementary school, he began to write poetry.

Langston had a gift for making others understand how black Americans lived, worked, talked, and played. People enjoyed his warm and funny writing style. Langston published his first poem, "The Negro Speaks of Rivers," after he graduated from high school. It is still one of his most popular poems.

Langston worked for a while in Washington, D.C., as a busboy. One day he put three of his poems beside the plate of a guest—a famous poet. The next day, newspapers around the country reported that a promising poet had been discovered. Soon, Langston had a scholarship to college. Before he graduated in 1929, he had published two books.

By the end of his life, Langston Hughes was one of America's finest writers. In 1960, the National Association for the Advancement of Colored People (NAACP) presented Hughes with the Spingarn Medal, declaring him "Poet Laureate of the Negro Race."

A Poet in Harlem

Langston Hughes loved to write. Tell about his writing and yours.

Name three things Langston Hughes wrote about.

_____
_____
_____
_____
_____
_____
_____
_____
_____
_____
_____
_____
_____
_____
_____
_____
_____
_____
_____
_____
_____
_____

Name three things you like to write about.

_____
_____
_____
_____
_____
_____
_____
_____
_____
_____
_____
_____
_____
_____
_____
_____
_____
_____
_____
_____
_____
_____

Marian Anderson
1897–1993

Marian Anderson was one of the greatest singers of her time. She came from a poor but close-knit family in Philadelphia. By the time she was six years old, she already had a beautiful voice. People were so excited when they heard her sing that they gave her money so she could have private voice lessons.

In 1925, Marian's voice teacher entered her in a contest with the New York Philharmonic Orchestra. Out of 300 contestants, she came in first place! She was invited to study music in Germany and took many tours through Europe.

While Marian was successful in Europe, she had to face people's racism in America. In February 1939, a big concert was planned at Constitution Hall in Washington, D.C. An important women's group did not want Marian to sing at the concert because she was black. Many famous people, including Eleanor Roosevelt, joined together to protest this decision.

As a result, Marian was invited by the U.S. government to sing in front of the Lincoln Memorial. On April 9, Easter Sunday morning, she sang for a crowd of 75,000 people. This event made Marian even more popular. Soon the whole country knew about her wonderful voice.

Marian Anderson received many great honors in her lifetime. Among them was the Presidential Medal of Freedom in 1963.

A Voice Loved around the World

Marian Anderson had an inspiring musical career. Write about important events that occurred in the beginning, middle, and end of her musical career.

Beginning

Middle

End

Duke Ellington
1899-1974

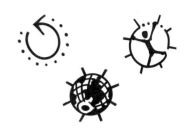

Edward Kennedy (Duke) Ellington was a great composer and musician. His special style of music made him famous around the world. He wrote jazz songs and orchestra music that influenced many other musicians.

Edward was born in Washington, D.C. At an early age, he showed unusual musical talent. He studied piano from the time he was seven years old. Sometimes he didn't like to practice, but he would do it anyway. His friends began to call him "Duke," because he liked to dress in fancy clothes.

At 17, music became Duke's full-time job. He was the leader of his own band in New York City and soon became a star. His music made people dance, smile, and cry. It helped people of different races come together.

Duke wrote more than 1,000 songs and composed music for films, operas, ballets, Broadway shows, and church services. *Sophisticated Lady* and *Satin Doll* are two of his most popular songs.

Duke Ellington received many awards in his life. His orchestra played for kings, queens, and presidents. His songs continue to delight millions of people today.

Duke Ellington Crossword Puzzle

Fill in the crossword puzzle using words that are part of Duke Ellington's life story. Use the Word Bank and the article for help.

Across

2. creative ability
5. someone who plays music
6. someone who writes music
9. the kind of music Duke played
10. one of Duke's most famous songs
12. the instrument Duke played

Down

1. a celebrity
3. Duke's last name
4. Edward Ellington's nickname
7. a large band
8. a musical group
11. musical tunes

Word Bank

band	composer	Duke
songs	orchestra	star
talent	musician	jazz
piano	Ellington	
Satin Doll		

National Association for the Advancement of Colored People

The National Association for the Advancement of Colored People (NAACP) was started in 1909. Its goal was to work for the fair treatment of African Americans. It was organized by W. E. B. Du Bois and 40 other people, both African-American and white. By 1955, the NAACP had more than 500,000 members.

The NAACP has most often fought its battles in court. Many of its cases have gone to the Supreme Court. In the beginning, the NAACP worked for African Americans who had been arrested or had been victims of illegal violence. Later, the organization worked for equality in education, housing, jobs, and voting rights for black people.

Many court cases argued by the NAACP changed history, but two stand out as landmarks. The first case involved a seven-year-old girl named Linda Brown. Her father sued the Board of Education of Topeka, Kansas. He wanted Linda to go to an all-white school in their neighborhood. At that time in Topeka, whites and blacks couldn't go to the same schools. The NAACP won the case. On May 17, 1954, the U.S. Supreme Court ruled that segregation in schools was illegal.

The second case occurred in 1955, when Rosa Parks refused to give up her bus seat to a white man in Montgomery, Alabama. At this time, segregation laws made it illegal for African Americans to sit next to whites on buses. When Rosa was arrested for not giving up her seat, the NAACP defended her in court. They won the case. On November 13, 1956, the justices of the Supreme Court decided that bus segregation laws were unconstitutional.

Today, the NAACP is still a leading civil rights organization. It continues to fight for justice and equality for all Americans.

The Work of the NAACP

Describe two court cases handled by the NAACP. Tell about the final decisions.

Case 1

_____
_____
_____
_____
_____
_____
_____
_____
_____
_____

Outcome

_____
_____
_____
_____
_____
_____
_____
_____
_____
_____

Case 2

_____
_____
_____
_____
_____
_____
_____
_____
_____
_____

Outcome

_____
_____
_____
_____
_____
_____
_____
_____
_____
_____

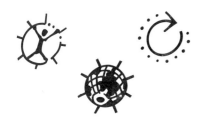

Thurgood Marshall
1908–1993

Thurgood Marshall cared about other people. When he practiced law, he represented many clients without getting paid for his work. He became the leading civil rights lawyer in the United States.

In 1938, Thurgood was named the top lawyer for the NAACP. He and his staff won 29 out of 32 Supreme Court cases. In 1946, he was honored with the Spingarn Medal.

Thurgood's most famous victory was in 1954, in the *Brown v. Board of Education* case. This was a time of segregation, when black and white children had to go to different schools. The case was named for Reverend Oliver Brown. His seven-year-old daughter, Linda, was not allowed to go to an all-white school just blocks from her home. Her father thought she should be allowed to attend. Marshall argued this case and won. For the first time in U.S. history, students of all races could go to the same schools. Segregated schools were now against the law.

In 1965, Thurgood was appointed Solicitor General of the United States. This means that he argued cases for the government in front of the Supreme Court. This was the highest law enforcement position ever held by an African American. When an opening occurred on the Supreme Court, President Lyndon B. Johnson nominated Thurgood for the position. In 1967, Thurgood Marshall became the first black justice of the United States Supreme Court.

Thurgood Marshall had a long and brilliant career as a Supreme Court justice. He retired in 1991. He is remembered as a great judge who dedicated his life to protecting the rights of all Americans.

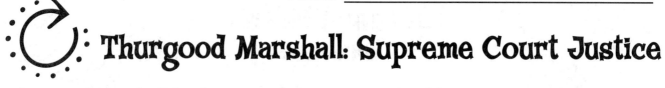

Thurgood Marshall: Supreme Court Justice

Thurgood Marshall had many achievements in his lifetime. Name the three achievements that you think are most important and tell why.

1. _____
   _____
   _____
   _____
   _____

2. _____
   _____
   _____
   _____
   _____

3. _____
   _____
   _____
   _____
   _____

Jesse Owens
1913–1980

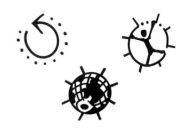

The 1936 Olympic games were held in Germany while the Nazis were in power. Adolf Hitler, the Nazi leader, said that Germans were a "master race." Many Germans believed him. They thought that Germans should rule the world. Hitler and his followers were sure that the Olympic games would prove they were right.

Jesse Owens came from a poor black family. He worked very hard in school and won a scholarship to Ohio State University. In college he became a track superstar.

In 1936, Jesse showed the world that he was a great athlete. In a blaze of glory, he won three Olympic gold medals—in the running broad jump, the 100-meter dash, and the 200-meter dash. His speed also helped his team win a gold medal in the 440-meter relay race. Jesse changed history by setting new world records.

These accomplishments made Adolf Hitler furious. A black man had embarrassed him in front of the world. Jesse Owens's success proved that people are winners because of their talent, not because of their race or nationality.

After retiring from track competition, Jesse Owens became a successful businessman, speaker, and youth worker. In 1976, he became the first black goodwill ambassador to the Olympic games. In the same year, he was honored with the Presidential Medal of Freedom.

A Blaze of Glory

Tell about Adolf Hitler's and Jesse Owens's plans for the 1936 Olympic games.
Were they the same or different? Tell what happened.

Adolf Hitler's plans for the 1936 Olympic Games

_____

_____

_____

_____

_____

Jesse Owens's plans for the 1936 Olympic Games

_____

_____

_____

_____

_____

What actually happened?

_____

_____

_____

_____

_____

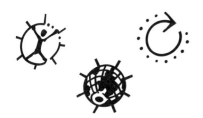

Shirley Chisholm
1924-2005

Shirley Chisholm was the first African-American woman elected to Congress. She helped change the country's feelings about women and African Americans.

Shirley was born in Brooklyn, New York. As a young girl, she lived with her grandparents on a farm in Barbados. Her grandmother taught her the values of courage, pride, and faith. After six years, Shirley returned to New York and attended a public school in Brooklyn. She graduated from Brooklyn College in 1946 and from Columbia University in 1952.

Shirley always loved children. Her first job was as a nursery school teacher. She soon became the director of a child-care center. Chisholm saw the problems of the poor every day. This led her to run for and win a seat in the New York State legislature.

Shirley Chisholm was small in size, but she proved to be a tough woman in politics. In 1969, she became the first black congresswoman in U.S. history. In Congress, she supported programs to improve inner-city life. She worked hard for more jobs, better education, and more daycare programs.

In 1972, Chisholm campaigned to be the Democratic nominee for president of the United States. She was the first black woman to do so. She did not win, but she did receive 152 votes at the convention. In 1993, she turned down President Bill Clinton's nomination to become ambassador to Jamaica due to poor health. Chisholm's hard work helped open the door for other African-American women in politics.

Name _____

First Black Congresswoman

What are some of the most significant events and accomplishments in Shirley Chisholm's life? Fill in the circle web with ideas from each category.

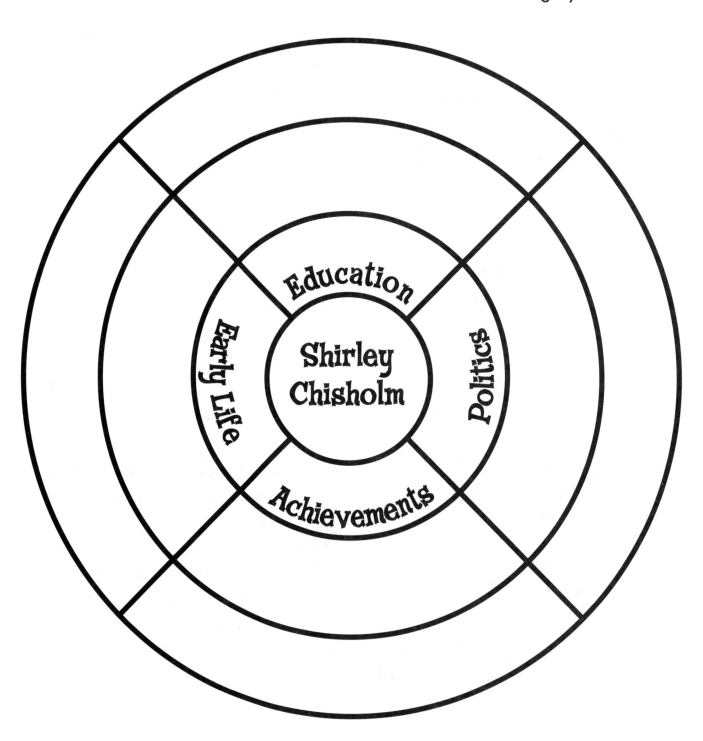

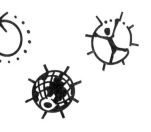

Martin Luther King, Jr.
1929-1968

In the 1960s, Martin Luther King's courage and leadership guided the civil rights movement.

Dr. King had three heroes—Martin Luther (the man for whom he was named), Henry David Thoreau, and Mohandas Gandhi. From their lives and teachings, Dr. King learned that nonviolent action was the best way to change unfair laws.

Martin was 25 years old when he chose to become pastor of a church in Montgomery, Alabama. He quickly impressed church members with his speaking and organization. Many of the people who went to his church knew he could be a great leader.

By 1955, Dr. King was a well-known and respected pastor. People looked to him to lead them in their campaign for civil rights. In 1956, he led the bus boycott that ended separate seating on Montgomery public buses.

One of the highlights of the civil rights movement was the March on Washington, D.C., in 1963. Dr. King led 250,000 people to the Lincoln Memorial to demand equality for all Americans. He called for support for President John F. Kennedy's civil rights bill. At the Lincoln Memorial, he made his famous "I Have a Dream" speech. A year later, Dr. King was awarded the Nobel Peace Prize.

On April 3, 1968, Dr. King went to Memphis, Tennessee. Garbage workers had asked him to help organize a protest march for fair pay. The next day, Dr. King was shot and killed. He was only 39 years old.

During his short life, Dr. King worked hard to secure equality and justice for all Americans. In 1983, a national holiday was declared to honor this great American. When we celebrate the birthday of Dr. Martin Luther King, Jr., we remember his inspiring dream.

Name _____

Martin Luther King, Jr.–Civil Rights Leader

Fill in the web with facts about Martin Luther King, Jr. Tell what you admire most about Dr. King.

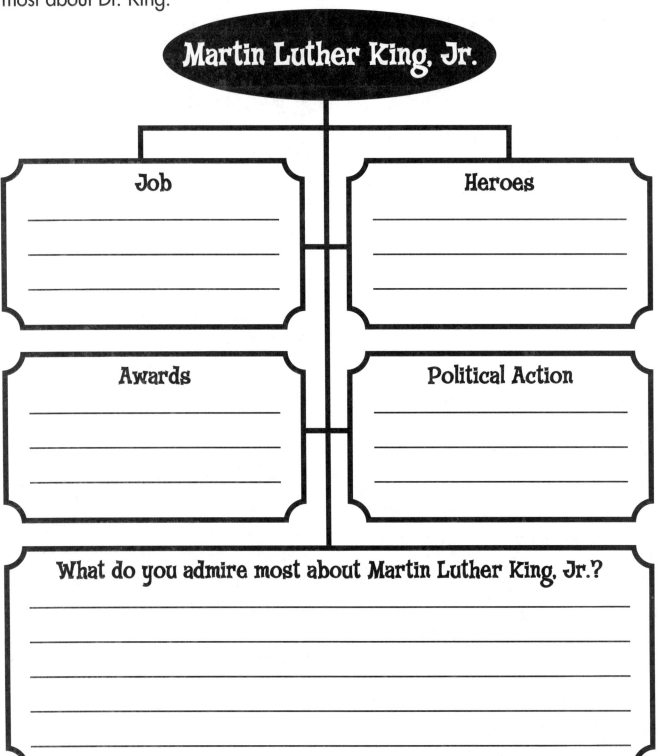

Martin Luther King, Jr.

Job

Heroes

Awards

Political Action

What do you admire most about Martin Luther King, Jr.?

Barack Obama
1961-

In the election of 2008, Barack Obama made history. He became the first African-American president of the United States. He would forever be known for opening new doors for people of color.

Barack was the child of a black father from Africa and a white mother from Kansas. His mother and grandparents raised him. The places where he grew up—Hawaii and Indonesia—also helped shape him. His experiences taught him to get along with many types of people.

Barack earned his degree from Columbia University in 1983. Then, he moved to Chicago. There, he worked with people who lived in poor areas. He wanted to make their lives better.

Law school at the famous Harvard University was next for Barack. After he graduated, he spent some time teaching and working as a lawyer. Then, he decided to enter the political world. Barack served in the Illinois Senate and then the U.S. Senate. He was only the third African American to be elected to the U.S. Senate.

Barack's Senate experiences prepared him for the next step in his career, a run for president of the United States. He competed with Hillary Clinton for the Democratic nomination. This was a historical moment in politics. It meant that either a woman or an African American had a real chance of becoming president.

Barack won the nomination. Next, he faced the Republican candidate John McCain. Barack's campaign was about hope, change, and bringing people together. He promised to bring American troops home from Iraq. He told Americans that they all deserved healthcare. He vowed to make decisions that would help slow global warming.

Americans liked what Barack Obama had to say. On November 4, 2008, they elected the first African-American president of the United States.

The First African-American President

Use the information in the selection to help you answer the questions about Barack Obama.

1. What do Barack's early life and career choices tell you about him as a person?

_____

_____

_____

_____

_____

2. What were some of the promises Barack made to Americans during his campaign?

_____

_____

_____

_____

3. Do you think it will be easier for people of other minorities to run for president in the future? Why or why not?

_____

_____

_____

Glossary

almanac—an annual publication containing an assortment of data, including weather and astronomical information

amendment—a change, sometimes to a bill or law

boycott—the organized effort of refusing to use or buy a product or service from another person, store, or country

candidate—a person who wants to hold an office or honor

civil rights—the rights of every citizen, regardless of color, race, gender, or religion

Civil War—the war between the North (the Union) and the South (the Confederacy) in the United States between 1861 and 1865

Constitution—the written set of basic principles that governs the United States

Emancipation Proclamation—a document signed by United States President Abraham Lincoln that freed many of the slaves

equality—the condition of having the same social, political, or economic rights

freedom—the liberty or power to do, say, or think as one pleases

invention—something made up or created

justice—fair treatment according to the law

law—a rule made by a government for all the people who live there

nonviolence—the practice of or belief in avoiding violence to accomplish one's goals

plantation—a large farm on which crops are grown and cared for by slaves who also live on the farm

protest—a gathering to show dislike or objection to something

racism—the practice of discriminating because of a person's race

revolt—an uprising or an act of rebellion against authority

runaways—people, especially slaves, who leave in order to escape to freedom

scholar—a person who has a great deal of knowledge

segregation—the separation of one racial group from a larger group or from the rest of society

Glossary

slavery—the condition of being owned by and forced to work for another person

Supreme Court—the highest court in the United States; Nine justices sit on this court.

transplant—to move from one body to another

unconstitutional—not in keeping with the principles of the constitution of a state or country

Underground Railroad—a system set up by people who helped runaway slaves in the South reach freedom in the North

Answer Key

Page 12
Across:
2. vision
3. bright
5. revolt
6. escape
7. dream
10. freedom
11. Virginia
12. slaves

Down:
1. liberate
4. preacher
8. arms
9. Turner

Page 34
Across:
2. talent
5. musician
6. composer
9. jazz
10. Satin Doll
12. piano

Down:
1. star
3. Ellington
4. Duke
7. orchestra
8. band
11. songs